I0842934

AGING BABY

KAREN KELLOCK PH.D.

**Manual for
Superior Men**

**A complete theory based on Einstein physics,
Political Psychology, Systems Theory
and Archetypal Psychiatry.**

FORMULA

**All success attraction
All disease obstruction
All recovery elimination**

**You must fast on all three
OBSTRUCTIONS:
People
Habit
Food**

AGING BABY

The boomers marked the beginning of mental and moral decline. They're so dumbed if you're too deep, all-encompassing, mystical, never heard before or not part o f narrative you're out of line. The enemy sows discord and division to the mob who can't discern good from evil. You're not even supposed to reason with fools yet that's the enemy's army against you. Don't envy when they flourish like a green tree for just as suddenly they're mowed down see.

MOB PSYCHOLOGY

GROUPTHINK & CONTAGION OF MADNESS
THE SENSITIVE CHILD CAN FEEL IT
YOU MUST EXPECT PERSECUTION
FALSELY ACCUSED, CHANGED FOREVER
WHEN THEY'RE ALL AGAINST YOU
TRUE INDEPENDENCE TAKES STRENGTH
THE SOCIAL WORLD IS VERY TAXING

MOB PSYCHOLOGY

GROUPTHINK & CONTAGION OF MADNESS

Anyone who's been the victim of groupthink [contagious madness] knows how it's entirely dangerous.

The mob is self-justifying. It moves like a flock of birds: according to each other not rational thinking.

You can be mobbed by your own family or by two or more against you: this is the cruel treachery.

The media can move the mob to do anything. They will believe what they hear, unquestioningly.

Even a young but sensitive child can read between the lines, he can feel what the mob decides.

THE SENSITIVE CHILD CAN FEEL IT

The sensitive child who "knows" what's happening will be punished accordingly for his seeing.

Any marginalized group develops a sixth sense about this buildup after what the media puts out.

This super-sensitivity is like an Indian in white man's territory. He feels what's happening, believe me.

If you expect persecution as a Christian it doesn't hurt so much & you can easily snap back friend.

If there wasn't a God we'd be totally forsaken facing the mob. It would fail with one against em all.

Expect this mob persecution as your special test. Expect it I say, then you'll win and can rest.

MOB PSYCHOLOGY

I never thought my own season of treason would ever end. God had special plans for me I guess.

YOU MUST EXPECT PERSECUTION

If I didn't expect horrible persecution and treachery I'd have extreme PTSD from all this you see.

Your frenemies were just doing the devil's bidding and it was all predictable esp. if you were sinning.

God's revenge on foes is delayed to ensure every last traitor plays their hand in your latter days.

Whenever persecuted or accused, think of all that Trump has experienced by the devil's crew.

Everyone should get a taste of what it's like to be falsely accused for it gives a new viewpoint too.

Instead of being pissed at what they did to you turn the anger on self for ever letting em in fool!

Be decent, law-abiding and a respected person of property and propriety then you're it sweetie.

Most modern women are empty pantsuits due to the sex revolution of the 60's making em fools.

FALSELY ACCUSED, CHANGED FOREVER

Once you've been falsely accused, mobbed and scapegoated you're changed for life, got it?

Accusations & indictments happen to the guilty and innocent alike. Just expect it in this life.

When falsely accused learn to stay calm. Don't throw a tantrum just join the ranks of great men.

MOB PSYCHOLOGY

It's usually jealousy that stimulates accusation then with the commoners it arouses suspicion.

They want to believe you're guilty because they just love having someone to scapegoat honey.

Be cautious in your season of treason. Don't drink or they'll shame you into jail or an institution.

WHEN THEY'RE ALL AGAINST YOU

When they're all against you it's the biggest thing to overcome, but remember IT CAN BE DONE.

Youth may not be able to relate to all this. But give it time and you'll know about it & be pissed.

You can be appreciating God's great earth then people come along and everything turns to worse.

It's hard to have boundaries if you were taught to be social--they even bring insults, you know?

Your traumatic experiences have shaped who you are. You'll always seek solitude & a closed door.

After having your boundaries busted & your true self disrespected you're changed forever, believe it.

You let em in: The trauma of busted boundaries all came from self-destructive tendencies.

You could have said NO but you didn't, all for social approval. It had to happen so you'd renew.

It takes a lot to come out of social hypnotism, it's like we gotta do what they want or somethin'.

It's like a compulsion or trance even tho' you hate every minute of it and want to escape the dance.

MOB PSYCHOLOGY

I know, boy do I know: I'm still suffering over the memories though it's been many years ago.

TRUE INDEPENDENCE TAKES STRENGTH

True independence takes such strength that few manage it, usually in latter years when aged.

Even then you may feel people imposing constantly, when firm boundaries make you feel guilty.

It's the human species: they're naturally groupies. But then you have the greats like geniuses see.

I recall the dismay being so happy alone & someone would come to the door to topple my throne.

If genius doesn't establish boundaries EARLY they'll spend half or more of life wasted, sadly.

It's been a social generation for fifty years, going beyond the mere groupie nature of humans/peers.

People drop by and you're expected to let em in. Before I had my great wall life was chaos and bedlam.

There is nothing so great as a WALL. Then it's your own little kingdom [queendom] and you rule it all.

THE SOCIAL WORLD IS VERY TAXING

Many don't even realize how taxing it is. They even think they like it: the social world of adults & kids.

In the fifties there was more respect for privacy but ever since then it's been stupid cruelty & treachery.

My contention is this has caused mental illness, which is a social illness--a mal-adaptation to all this.

It's the basis to all my books: mental illness is a social illness, for left alone we wouldn't get hooked.

SMILING DICTATORS

IT'S ALL SOCIAL HYPNOTISM
FRIENDS WITH DIFFERENT VALUES
MISALLIGNED VALUES WRECK YOUR PEACE
BETRAYAL BY FRIENDS AND FAMILY
DON'T EVEN TRY TO ARGUE WITH EM
THEY FALL INTO THE PIT LIKE LEMMINGS
COLLECTIVE MADNESS
HOW COULD THEY BE SO DUMB?
COMMIE DICTATORS SMILE
TYRANTS INVADING YOUR HOME
THE DICTATORS WEAR A SMILE
PRAY FOR HELP IN THE NAME OF JESUS
TRAUMA BRINGS IMPLODED BOUNDARIES
RAPE AND PLUNDER IS ALL OVER
WHERE ARE THEY NOW? THEY'RE ALL GONE
YOUR COMEBACK: LYMPHATIC DRAINAGE

SMILING DICTATORS

IT'S ALL SOCIAL HYPNOTISM

Why do they think the way they do? Because their FRIENDS do: they're the social hypnotic crew.

They hate Trump because "they" hate Trump. They call him a racist cuz "they" do; that's all it is.

Social hypnosis is a contagion of madness. It's like a virus: all the commoner lame brains get it.

A woman is hurt, her self-esteem plunges and she becomes more reckless as life deranges.

The "poor" man is not one who has little but one who craves more. Streamline for joy evermore.

FRIENDS WITH DIFFERENT VALUES

A friend with different values wrecks your tranquility. Do they just drop by when you love privacy?

Discomfort and tension is too high a price to pay for the supposed joy & validation of being "social" ok.

You must always reflect on associations to ensure they promote your moral & personal growth son.

Recognizing these misaligned values is crucial for your internal harmony and continued growth see.

Don't you want tranquility and continuous happiness? Then it's essential to have the same values sis.

What you're doing is establishing an environment where you can thrive, produce and create, amen!

SMILING DICTATORS

Your home is the ONE place you can choose your own circumstances--not the world, ruled by chance.

Do you have colleagues who prioritize personal gain over collaboration? That's another problem.

MISALLIGNED VALUES WRECK YOUR PEACE

You must notice & correct these things or pay the piper later, with things like waking up in anger.

Open conversations about the problem may help but if different values remain, you must get out.

When core values clash with those around you, life is hell and you gotta fix the problem Sue.

Recognizing misaligned values and taking ACTION to address them is essential for well being son.

Let each hardship fortify a resolve to be great. Let em harden you, build social muscle & routine ok.

The second verse is the same as the first. Once rid of the curse if you let it back in it will be worse.

BETRAYAL BY FRIENDS AND FAMILY

The saddest thing about betrayal is it never comes from your enemies but from a friend's treachery.

You always thought differently from the rest. Not part of the herd mentality, you needed protection sis.

You can't argue them into true reality, just know YOU have the truth and ignore the herd mentality.

Watch movies, sit in the sun, read a book: anything but listen to them, the smiling hoods and crooks.

SMILING DICTATORS

Their reality is so psychotic & wrong you must hold onto your head by not attending to the throng.

Of course they call YOU psychotic and wrong but that's part of the obstacle you must overcome.

DON'T EVEN TRY TO ARGUE WITH EM

Don't argue with em, that's the worst thing you can do. It's a mental illness so just get back into YOU.

You hear friends & family spouting the false line. Don't argue, they too have fallen into the pit, aye.

You cannot talk any more sense into them than you could a psycho mental illness patient, amen.

Save yourself and protect your OWN sanity by staying away and not even visiting their pages ok.

I know it's mind-numbing & hurts like hell when friends sink into swill but it's history repeating still.

You can't do anything about it but wave goodbye while you're at it and just pray they finally get it.

But if you attend to what they say you are in danger of losing your own sanity and very life ok.

THEY FALL INTO THE PIT LIKE LEMMINGS

I've watched many friends & family fall like gremlins following the smiling, fawning peanut gallery.

Don't let it ruin your day. Read a book, take a long nap or warm bath, treat yourself like gold today.

As you see the other side lying about everything & accusing you of what THEY do, JUST RENEW.

SMILING DICTATORS

Instead of fighting with the enemy, be gentle with yourself for this is serious stuff & you need help.

It's a horrible plight you're in but it's an historical pattern of Satan. You just overcome it friend.

The false accusations & blatant lies come so fast and furious you feel delirious but now, JUST REST.

Realize how mind-numbing this is but you can't afford a blitz so simply focus on self-gentleness.

COLLECTIVE MADNESS

I watched people I'd known all my life fall into the pit of collective madness so I know this sadness.

I was astonished, enraged and wanted to argue but that only made em more mentally obdurate too.

It's like Hitler's Germany or Mao's China all over again, when God's people said goodbye to friends.

Social hypnotism is stronger than loyalty to family or friends, history has shown this over again.

And when evil gets control of the media, it's over for sure. People believe what they hear, a lure.

When they accuse you of the most absurd things, just crawl into bed for a nap or take a warm bath.

Save the energy drain: don't argue with the fray but focus on keeping your tranquility/brain ok.

HOW COULD THEY BE SO DUMB?

You think: "how could they be so dumb?" but that is how human social hypnotism works hon'.

SMILING DICTATORS

They believe it because all their friends believe it and the bought media confirms it: THAT'S IT.

COMMIE DICTATORS SMILE

Commies are always smiling, that's part of their gimmick. They're the smiling dictators: sick.

All commie regimes shout "JOY!" with happy faces on posters but the reality is just the opposite sirs.

Good leaders are far more serious cuz there's so much to do. These are conservatives who help you.

Liberals won't talk of the issues just "joy, joy, joy" to convert you but it's all bull so wake up Sue.

Commie dictators have the best smile and that's how dumb they think you are: easily beguiled.

They smile as they turn the knife in your back: that's the "progressives" which are backward in fact.

They beguile you thru actors, singers and anyone famous and rich while you fall into a ditch.

Conservatives love God, family and country but liberals only care about a woe-begotten theory.

The worst dictators in the world ruling the poorest countries have only posters with smiles see.

TYRANTS INVADING YOUR HOME

Example: Tyrants invading your home always say how good they are while having nothing to offer.

What I've learned in the my long life is watch out for smiling dictators and particularly the "nice".

SMILING DICTATORS

I had to learn all this the hard way, thinking I was popular letting them into my house ok.

Your house should be inviolate, a sacred sanctuary for just you and yours not a bunch of users.

They with nothing better to do coming to bother you are the problems Sue so get a wall or be screwed.

If you don't have a wall around you you're a weasel with a sign: "come and take advantage now", aye.

THE DICTATORS WEAR A SMILE

They're like a smiling well-dressed waiter with a dirty kitchen behind him. It's all a ruse friend.

The most important part of the house is the fence, so they can't come to the door to menace.

See your friendly home invaders as a boat with a hole in it: of course the water will come in it.

The whole world wants to come in your house. You keep things so nice and you got good chow.

They treat you like a free country club or club house to come hang out. It's their place to go--ouch!

Free drinks, smokes and whatever you got cooking. Think of it: they show up at lunch don't they?

Cast off the works of darkness and put on the armor of light. That's how you handle PTSD, alright?

Not having boundaries is like a boat with a hole in it: the water [scammers, intruders] will come in, get it?

He'll stay with you as long as he gets what HE wants. It's not about you girls, get that thru your heads.

SMILING DICTATORS

He'll stay with you as long as he gets what HE wants. It's not about you girls so drop that scuzz.

Without boundaries you're nothing but a boat with a hole in it so of course you'll be flooded.

PRAY FOR HELP IN THE NAME OF JESUS

Ultimately the only cure for constant PTSD intrusive thoughts is Jesus. GOD replaces em all, I promise.

I tried everything to stop intrusive thoughts but the groove kept getting deeper until God appeared.

I was harassed by my thoughts for decades: things that could not be corrected until God gave aid.

If you're a boat with a hole in it {boundariless] AND in sin it's like a magnet bringing evil floods in.

This helps with PTSD: it was YOU causing the problem because due to sins your hedge was down.

If in sin you've no one to blame but yourself when wicked men creep in: it's like a magnet to them.

All the fretting, sign-making and anguish about my PTSD when all I had to do was ask God see.

I poured my heart out about my violated boundaries and God took it all away in an instant ok.

TRAUMA BRINGS IMPLODED BOUNDARIES

One result of trauma is imploded boundaries--our hedge is down. Even our friends wear a frown.

When our own friends and family turn their heel against us it's hellish. We let it all happen, in anguish.

SMILING DICTATORS

When we come around, vindication is necessary for the relief of the saints. We'll see it the book says.

It's like wild birds eating our flesh and we are helpless. When up again they're not just embarrassed.

When down they come in and take everything, it's like a compulsion of demonic powers in em see.

They're like old women coming in after death to take what's left. When back up it's hard forgetting it.

RAPE AND PLUNDER IS ALL OVER

Rape and plunder was what it was. It was like taking candy from a baby in a country without laws.

Now you've repented & come to your senses God vindicates His kids punishing these offenses.

He lays out a banquet for you after coming home and your foes must see it, that's what I know.

When up again you can't believe what happened. Their sins are glaring and God's wrath is smokin'.

When you were vulnerable and down in that state, principalities and powers took over the irate.

WHERE ARE THEY NOW? THEY'RE ALL GONE

Where are these ugly foes now? They are dead or toothless. You look but can't find the lawless.

Purified & repentant you're as pure as a baby: your plunderers must face what they did see.

They had their fun but now you're up again. They must face they killed a saint and it's hell on em.

SMILING DICTATORS

When the hedge is down without God's protection you can't help yourself: that's how it is son.

The weasels invaded your home & took all you had, I know. It like demons came up from below.

When their false accusations & blaming kept coming there was nothing you could do when sinning.

Only repentance brings back the armor of God, so that it all turns around and you're back on top.

YOUR COMEBACK: LYMPHATIC DRAINAGE

A wife tells if he's lost interest or distracted. If it's raining she's more stressed then that starts it.

She may eat AT it then loses attractiveness. When his interest lessens this downturn increases.

No facelifts necessary, just clean lymph thoroughly. That's all I gotta say re: the science of beauty.

Eliminating allergies [restricting foods] thins the face. It's like a mini facelift as the lymph drains ok.

EMPATHS & TRUTHTELLERS

GREAT PEOPLE FEEL ISOLATED
CHARACTER ASSASSINATION
THEY CAN'T EVEN CONSIDER HIS VIEWS
ALTERING OR WITHHOLDING INFORMATION
BUILDING AN INDEPENDENT SELF
PAIN PRECEDES GREAT GLORY & JOY
MUST CHURCHES ARE SOCIAL HALL RELIGION
THE OUTER LIFE: LONELY AND BORED
HOW TO HANDLE POLI-PSYCHO FRIENDS
THEY ARE SO ARROGANT
SAVE YOURSELF THRU FORGIVENESS
THE NECESSITY OF RELOCATION
COMMONERS WORSHIP EACH OTHER
JUST PUT EM ALL IN A BAG

EMPATHS & TRUTHTELLERS

GREAT PEOPLE FEEL ISOLATED

Anyone great feels misunderstood by the world around him. It's like a tidal wave, it's overwhelmin'.

Every great discoverer in history had to go against the grain, like 10,000 were against him ok.

They're so used to having multitudes around and they take their social reality as truth, that's all.

It can be overwhelming to the truth-teller with an indescribable pressure to go along with the herd.

This constant pressure isolates them more until they're in total solitude--what others can't endure.

CHARACTER ASSASSINATION

Scapegoats, empaths and truthtellers face character assassination by their own families son.

A scapegoat is like a stigma: they see everything he does but with anyone else no one sees ya.

They will protect the status quo with you as scapegoat and them as the in-crowd: it's hell below.

As long as you stay down they don't have to look at their own issues, so simply put: you're screwed.

They'll do anything and tell any lie to keep that system in place and it's hell on earth for you ok.

Just to exist a scapegoat shares things going against the family's malignant normalcy: that poor kid.

EMPATHS & TRUTHTELLERS

The toxic family must shut him down for it's just too painful and difficult to consider this clown.

THEY CAN'T EVEN CONSIDER HIS VIEWS

To reconsider the views of the scapegoat compels looking at other views they have--so **NO**.

It's about cognitive dissonance: "don't confuse me with the facts" so he's kept down to the max.

The family's "superself" of identity--groupthink, malignant normalcy--is rigidly maintained see.

The superself is a programmed way of thinking shoved down the throats of even the extended family.

The major premise of the superself makes the scapegoat **NOT FIT** so he's disbelieved: illigit.

The scapegoat is banned and shunned cuz he's not carrying the party line, just like Trump: aye.

The scapegoat's claims if true would bring repercussions on the crew so he's pooh-poohed.

The flow of information [the grapevine] is controlled to manipulate the truthteller: denial forever.

ALTERING OR WITHHOLDING INFORMATION

By **ALTERING** or withholding information the group maintains its interests which are rigidly fixed.

In the narcissistic system information is power and currency, just like the lamestream news see.

When system abuse of the target is normalized, anyone questioning it will be thrown out or despised.

EMPATHS & TRUTHTELLERS

The normalization of mistreatment goes to absurd levels until revealed and accepted by the right people.

There's a lack of tangible proof of scapegoating as they don't leave clear footprints of their doings.

There's a lack of a smoking gun even tho' the culprit's standing there in clear sight as favorite son.

The scapegoat always has to argue "beyond reasonable doubt". I wrote 98 books about it to get out.

BUILDING AN INDEPENDENT SELF

He must build a self not based on what others think but who he really IS. It's a tremendous feat sis.

Believing in yourself despite what **ALL** others think is biblical: despite being hated by 10,000 people.

Stop trying to change others into believing you're the wronged scapegoat. Our slogan: let em go!

Focus on strengthening your emotional immune system: "I don't care what you think" will be it, amen.

You must become **IMMUNE** to their irrational way of seeing you or themselves. Built that wall!

You must release with love or hate: detachment. You've been programmed just as they have: shun it.

Tho' you've been rejected, shamed and blamed you can change this matrix and find yourself, a saint.

PAIN PRECEDES GREAT GLORY & JOY

Always remember: The pain you're feeling can't compare to the joy that's coming. Romans 8: 18

EMPATHS & TRUTHTELLERS

Why do people drink double at high school reunions? Because people are mean seeing you again.

You meet an old friend and see alcohol's the most important thing in their lives: home again.

They know nothing and see nothing. But alcohol keeps em together on a daily basis [it's startling].

It seems everyone's been divorced. What used to be a rare thing shows on their faces for the worst.

Everyone's experienced something awful. We used to be peaceful but now PTSD shows on people.

They cover it over & mal-adapt thru drinking or drugging. They are zombies & care about nothing.

You become a majority of one, lonely but dependent on none. If fortunate you found God and won.

Usually the vision quest and solitude happens in old age but with me it happened early: a sage.

I got so sick of people invading and grifting me I relocated and established a new life happily.

Fortunately I was married but had lived decades alone as a solitary, escaping the social sillies.

MUST CHURCHES ARE SOCIAL HALL RELIGION

I loved God but hated social hall religion which most had become. Loving GOD should be number one.

If you need people you will need them more but enjoy them less. This is the life of the majority sis.

They are frantic to maintain contact since they have no inner life to fall back on, to live and express.

EMPATHS & TRUTHTELLERS

They think loving people is godly and show it in their maudlin fakery. It's a joke to the truly mature see.

They feel popular and confirmed if people drop by constantly, never knowing what they're missing.

To think of the hours, weeks and months wasted putting up with drop-by's & goals distracted.

No matter how lettered & honored these people are lonely & bored cuz they don't have the Lord.

THE OUTER LIFE: LONELY AND BORED

It's all an OUTER life while real life is an INNER one. They keep you from that, stealing your life hon'.

You get addicted to people too easily. First they bug you then you adapt & want them to call see.

Being snubbed at an early age leaves a mark on your face & some wear it until their latter days.

The upper lip curls up in contempt after held down as a kid: a look of defiance and being pissed.

First you hate it when they come then you mal-adapt and then when they leave you cry, what fun.

When you think differently from the whole world it feels like a tidal wave coming in on you girls.

HOW TO HANDLE POLI-PSYCHO FRIENDS

How to handle politically naive friends: know they're hypnotized and you can't do a thing, amen.

Instead of stewing with frustration & resentment over political naive friends it's best to forget em.

EMPATHS & TRUTHTELLERS

Due to this politically charged atmosphere they will not change depending on the news they watch ok.

It's two parallel news universes and they're not getting the news you get and won't listen dearest.

It's alarming when friends seem so incredibly naive but that's hypnotism so learn your lesson see.

It must have been alarming in Hitler's Germany when friends went dark and became so arrogant.

The same poli-psycho process is happening here and there's nothing you can do about it dears.

THEY ARE SO ARROGANT

They seem so arrogant in their ignorance and they hang together in a flock which makes it worse.

They hang together in self-congratulatory ignorance and then there's you in your separateness.

I know what it's like when the whole world is crazy and you're alone, banned, scorned in treachery.

People you knew all your life have turned their heel against you, part of the herd of mind-screwed.

I know dear one, I know. Now stick with your own kind, a wide world separated from those below.

SAVE YOURSELF THRU FORGIVENESS

You must SAVE yourself dear one, from your naive and hypnotized friends or you'll be the sick one.

Don't argue with them anymore. Block them: it's entirely useless trying to change the hardcore.

EMPATHS & TRUTHTELLERS

They think it's racist not wanting millions to invade the country. Isn't that hardcore ya think honey?

So let em go, they'll be swept into hell like the rest of godless humanity listening to such folderol.

Think of your crazy friend as hardcore and there's nothing you can do to change him or her.

THE NECESSITY OF RELOCATION

There are demons surrounding a whole town that becomes a strong hold. Relocate to make gold.

Stay there and be hated or relocate and be loved. It happens immediately from angels above.

Don't hate your ex-friend, just see it as a poli-"psycho" process seen throughout history, amen.

People come and go, so don't get addicted to anyone you know. Let em go, get back into the flow.

COMMONERS WORSHIP EACH OTHER

The commoners worship each other. They don't know the Lord and don't care to know Him either.

If they're that dumb--subscribing to all the crap under the sun--let em go and have your own fun.

They're always surrounded by smiling friends while you're always alone wishing for the same.

This is the plight of God's men and women: alone in faith though ten thousand are against em.

Seeing your naive brainwashed friends in this light allows you to forgive em, so you can go on.

EMPATHS & TRUTHTELLERS

As long as you're angry at em or feeling separate and forlorned you can't go on or be happy hon'.

JUST PUT EM ALL IN A BAG

Just put em all in a bag just as you do bad memories. Now throw it out and go on ahead sweetie.

You can't believe they think as they do. I know, I was that way too but forgiveness ends the feud.

Good people in Nazi Germany watched with dismay as friends went along: see this as a lesson.

It is profitable to take a Mother Theresa stance: love them as little children needing educatin'.

As long as you're In a feud things don't go well for you dude. Love em as crazy kids though rude.

It's hard when the brainwashed arrogantly act intellectually superior but you must forget it dear.

It gets violent or ugly at times: the pressure to conform. Can you comfortably go against the norm?

ONE ALKALINE MEAL A DAY FOR SENSITIVES

Go lowcarb if you want but it's totally acidic. For my system I need alkaline so the lymph can drain it.

Lowcarb may bring beauty at first but the acidity will catch up on you and you'll age quickly see.

I need one meal a day of nutritive-dense carbs and veg with some protein: it's alkaline & energizing see.

What I learned is: a smiley good-looker could still have bad character. Never judge on appearances sir.

EMPATHS & TRUTHTELLERS

If you want low weight like I do, every day has to be a fast past break-fast. One meal a day dearest.

No snacks later either. Just ONE MEAL sister, that's if you want low-weight like a true discoverer.

Due to the chemical incursion all around, you easily get round if you eat more than that I've found.

I eat a large meal around 5 am then I have all day to digest it, fasting for the high life & lovin' it.

TRUISMS THAT WILL HEAL YOUR HURT

Truth is still truth tho' no one believes it, a lie is still a lie tho' everyone believes it. Truism

The older I get the more I live a life others don't or can't understand and that's totally ok man.

Compare heaven with human society. Just being with God and angels not this kind of snobbery.

Old age is luxury. "What the caterpillar calls the end the Master calls a butterfly" -Richard Bach

FIND SOMEONE SAFE

If it's a virtual pal don't go back to his channel. You'll just get hurt cuz that's his ego level.

The abused victim can't see the pattern: that love is always followed by discard and devaluin'.

Don't worry, the narcissist will bring himself down. It's inevitable because that's the pattern.

PRIDE BEFORE THE FALL

Pride goeth before the fall Father, You have said so. That guys is arrogant: he's NOT humble.

Pride goeth before the fall Father, You have said so. So why reward my enemy who's so unhumble?

When a friend becomes insufferable what are you to do? Don't suffer seeing them any more Bro'

What happens to the narcissist as he ages? He gets worse in all the above characteristics.

Hold your head up high and stick your nose up in the air if you have to. Never cave in, remain YOU.

Just wait: Jesus said those who exalt themselves will be humbled but the humble will be exalted.

Since their symptoms are exacerbated towards the end, narcs become insufferable as friends.

Control your thoughts. Don't ALLOW them to go to "him". This will bring great elation my friend.

Make yourself entirely happy: control your thoughts and actions. It's all in your camp: block him.

FIND SOMEONE SAFE

SEXUAL MARKET VALUE: POOH!

Don't give a dam about "SMV": your sexual market value. You're part of the Kingdom of God Sue.

Any man talking about SMV: drop him immediately cuz your value is extremely high to God see.

Lying and playing people against each other: ever wonder why he hurts you this way dear?

If success hits and he shows insufferable arrogance see the glitch and keep your distance.

SICKNESS FROM THE NARCISSIST

NOTICE: How seeing him brings you down but no-contact--selfhood--brings great elation.

Gut aches: triangulation, manipulation, siding against, false accusation, disrespect, gossip.

So you got him, how you gonna keep him? Cuz that's the problem as things get boring/ho hum.

Because he's so desperately empty he'll hoover you back, that's a fact, only to be sacked.

It's all about him, not you--remember that. It's not you he wants but your function as supply, the rat.

Cruel cruel cruel, as cruel as he can be, having no empathy and compelled to envy/treachery.

You fear your final foot-down will bring volatile vindictive revenge but you've got God now.

IDEALIZE THEN DEVALUE/DUMP

FIND SOMEONE SAFE

Narcissism IS: to idealize you but then, inevitably, to devalue and discard you. You need healing Sue.

I know he appeals but don't take a chance, don't go back. You're about to find your SELF intact.

The damage this person has done is heavier than you know. Time bombs erupt later from long ago.

It's trigger, trigger, trigger--sparks going off every time you hear him. Why? You sense manipulation.

YOU CAN'T HOLD HIM

Let him go cuz he'll be gone anyway if it's up to him. You can't tame this thing/it's dangerous see.

I've been down this path drenched in chemicals--adrenalin and cortisol--then a terrible fall.

It's having the rug pulled out constantly. Of dealing with shock and disappointment regularly.

He scares you with his stuff: that's been the lure, a chemical hit of excitement then dumped.

Don't think of the rush--think only the hangover after, like a drunk. Recall ONLY THAT or flunk.

When he says he loves you he means that's how he feels today but tomorrow? It goes away.

It's a dangerous world so find a safe man. A humble man not so into looks, image or deceptions.

You want a man you can rely on. And I'm speaking emotionally since that's the female basically.

Cut him off then take a walk. Get into details of the earth, expand your mind, decide your wants.

FIND SOMEONE SAFE

As you exchange your own reality for thoughts of him a cornucopia explodes inside, God's blessin'!

Suddenly the sun, moon, stars and sand explode in your senses and you have arrived my sistas.

As "he" recedes a new vista opens to queens. Obsession/unrequited love are terrible feelings.

You feel outa his league but actually he's outa your league. Don't take this on, walk tall/free.

Does he pay the bills? Does he solve problems and give protection? That's all you need woman.

CRAZY WITH EMOTIONAL UPS/DOWNS

Does he make you crazy with emotional ups and downs or allow your femininity to be glowin'?

Seek PEACE in your home life, for that is our natural niche: HOME is all to a queen, not a witch.

He's like a little boy who needs his face slapped. But he can't learn a thing, he is recalcitrant.

Humans become more individualized--unique--in eldering anyway, not so much inter-relating see.

They are always caught in their own net. That's a given so just wait it out and God will vindicate it.

Body is a water well--blood circulating thru each cell--so overnight the wrinkled become beautiful.

The extreme ectomorph is a hyper-evolute: further along yet they say "don't get too thin woman".

We need far more protein as we age. May I suggest cheese? It's just as proteinized as meat.

GETTING UNSTUCK

GETTING UNSTUCK

DOWNPUTTING FORCES

Staying high despite forces trying to bring you down, that's the rite of knights in this generation.

Either take the reins and own power or be the victim of false accusation in this evil hour.

The fascination of Social Psychology is the Herd: how it can be moved, swerved and triggered.

In my early immaturity I was so vulnerable to praise bombing I was a sitting duck for smarties.

It's not he's rejecting you, he just can't rise to the task. You can't see it but he's a loser/low class.

You go thru hard times but then everything returns to the beginning--unless you keep sinning.

To be beset by PTSD memory or besot by a rogue due to early tragedy is the immaturity.

COLLAPSED BOUNDARIES: "EASY"

She was "easy" due to collapsed boundaries and lack of moral instruction or good examples see.

If he hurt you don't ever be at his mercy again by going to his channel or anything else friend.

Traumatized, boundaries collapse. Then your whole world goes to hell as your hedge is trashed.

You're too old to cry over family. BE the family for the world of rejected anomalies.

GETTING UNSTUCK

The last stage of life is sovereign independence, usually a breakaway before ascendance.

It's called "eldering" and its freedom and release from structure to find the self/wisdom.

AUTONOMY is a major concept in psychology and it's the stage of bliss and freedom see.

LEVELING FORCES

The more they invalidate and gaslight you the better they feel about themselves too.

As an elder you recall how people took up your time, rained on your parade and crashed your sails, aye.

But when enmeshed in social systems you can't see how they degraded and used you ma'am.

Note to Champs: Maybe they're smart enough to see it/maybe not, so be it--you did the job.

A human tsunami came in on me and I was blamed for all of it. The season of treason is pure treachery.

Most fired up ambition is to change opinion about him by dead ancestors/introjection?

MAKE THE PAST DEAD INSTEAD

A man's greatest achievement is to put the past behind him and happily go on. Paul

Female gossip got people thrown into concentration camps and women aren't dangerous?

Her vicious tongue is her armory, her flying monkeys ready for battle on her enemies.

GETTING UNSTUCK

You can't talk a liberal out of it if he gets enough support from others to support it.

FAME VS. STAYING HIDDEN

It's your choice: fame for uniqueness or staying down with the masses being abused for this.

In the interim: frustrated being hidden yet terrified of being in the middle or ever seen again.

If there's one thing I've learned in my life it's things can turn in a second tho' you're in the right.

People are cruel, children are most cruel. You gotta be defensive in this life and ready to school.

You're only young once but immature you can always be. In fact few people ever have maturity.

The power of the group over the individual is tyrannical but claustrophobic to an intellectual.

DON'T ASSOCIATE WITH FOOLS

Some are raised to be great--to expand their boundaries/envision their future bounties.

One sign of a good person: he won't associate with a fool because he'll pull him down with him.

When you've finally [fortunately] outgrown the obsession then let him go now and be done.

I outgrew obsession and he started fading. Hurray, I was escaping as a new vista was opening.

They have flashes of brilliant charisma but then they lose it and don't know how to repair flaws.

GETTING UNSTUCK

You gotta work on self on how to spring back cuz we all go dense at times: how to return to high.

I outgrew obsession and finally saw him: a rather nondescript person, a really big nothin'.

NOTICE FREQUENT FICKLENESS

He loves you today but someone else tomorrow. Keep this in mind: see things through time gal.

You fascinate him today but tomorrow it's another lady and you don't even come to his mind ok.

The most energetic become the biggest sinners. Change the premise and they're biggest winners.

You know ONE thing about him: he's fickle as hell and you'd truly suffer with such an infidel.

No more suffering over fickle: you must now choose and be ATTRACTED to the reliable.

Signs of a new gal: She is now attracted to the reliable, not the flashy irresponsible.

Everyone should want ONE whom they can trust: this is a marriage and having a spouse.

It's hard wading thru the dross to get to the diamond. The nice guy in the back, he's your man.

CLEARING THE MIND

Your problem is clearing the mind not adding more stuff to it: simplify the scene to intuit.

What is mental illness? Traumatized and not worked thru--shit in the system that's what it is.

GETTING UNSTUCK

No looking back, no turning to salt. Relapse into salt and you'll start looking back--it's s rut.

BORN INTO AN UNDERTOW

Many became great in their field after working their problems out. It's obstruction, a rut.

You go through a LOT in life then take what you've learned to help others-- what else is there.

Here's the thing kids: it takes audacity, boldness--but you gotta repent to get this.

They stomped on the gas and now they've got chaos. Patience is a fruit, I'm telling you folks.

A rat is the lowest thing you could be but to fight women wreck reputations constantly.

Born clear, we meet an undertow: we're broken kings and queens lest we overcome the fiends.

Salvaged identity: Women wanna see their visage in the heavens, that's what fame means to them.

BREAKING THE QUEEN

They wanna break the queen into female slave consciousness. Since WWII this is the matrix.

Eldering is about looking back and making gold from lucid gems. It's a blast and revisioning.

Sin dissolves your hedge of protection. The evil world flows in: life becomes hellish/you're done.

A liberal mother will not give moral instruction by definition, it's too huge a contradiction.

FASCINATION OF SOCIAL PSYCHOLOGY

GETTING UNSTUCK

The fascination of Social Psychology is the Herd: how it can be moved, swerved and triggered.

They make their move, the public reacts and activism is called off--but illegalization follows fast.

Political theater needs a script, a list of enemies and it's own events to galvanize the elect.

Information bubble defined: You only listen to info from your own, not the opposite side.

I look at wars as a social psychologist. It's about the forces of herds as each other they convince.

The worst thing about news: how they mix important with trivial, pork with quintessential.

Retirement means: music, musing and movies [fascinating historical documentaries].

Not so much news. it's repeat, fillers and narratives tho' I love evocative commentaries too.

ANTITRUMPISM AND TDS

You should've been honored but were treated like a common criminal and menace. God to Trump

GNP was never higher, taxes never lower, border secure--but they hate him like a murderer.

The night of terror was long and frightening but it too must come to a close/it all changed see.

Anything seems possible when you don't know what you're talking about. John Kennedy

IS THE PROBLEM SALT OR SUGAR?

GETTING UNSTUCK

Addicted to salt I desired all spicy foods. After de-salting the body that was all gone too.

The story of Lot talks of salt statues. It turns the body to concrete: hardened patches you can see.

Sugar isn't the problem, it is SALT. The world's instant addiction when they found it, a poison!

Salty, fatty things I was addicted to. It's most delicious but destroys your appearance too.

Desiccated, flaky/patchy tissues = SALT! Productive coughing from water retention = SALT!

Lungs were perfect after pot smoking but SALT created water retention--/phlegm/coughing.

Salt: scratchy dry lungs with superfluous water [phlegm] flowing thru there, yuk!

Some say 80% of women are on anti-depressants seen as "happy pills" but they depress you girls.

When it comes to pot chewables, just a lick. Don't ever ingest the whole thing you hick.

To me, eggs smell like--well, I don't even wanna say it. Like a barn or sulphur from a sewer plant.

After all this vegan stuff for decades I prefer ice cream sundays and I've never felt/looked better ok.

God made delicious olives and anchovies but He didn't make things like macaroni and cheese.

JUST SKIP DINNER

It's like a continuous Ramadan fast without dinner. Breakfast only plan before dawn = winner.

GETTING UNSTUCK

No digestion during daylight is a great high dividing the day that way--it's rigid discipline, aye.

Have the dishes washed and teeth brushed by the business day and now **FAST** for success ok.

Never be seen eating, it is degrading. Elites stay high above the masses always stuffing.

You're too old to whine about family: BE that shining star that relies on God only.

You're now a flawless individual molded out of purity, piety, energy and strength of character.

Our birthday probably has archetypal power, like starting a new cycle. It always makes me thoughtful.

AGING BABY

PRIMED FOR MADNESS
THRIVE THOUGH THEY HATE YOU
DIRTY OLD MEN [HIPPIES]
DIRTY JOKES IN THE HOME
JUST ASKING YOU GROW UP
NARCISSIST SH*T TESTS
NARCISSISTS NEVER WANT CLOSURE
WEAK WOMEN LET EM IN
CHARM ISN'T CHARCTER
HE'S LIKE A SLOT MACHINE
CUED UP BY ORIGINAL TEMPLATES
FOES DO THEMSELVES IN IF YOU DON'T
EMOTIONS SPLINTER THE MIND
LOW STRESS MARRIAGE: "HONEY"
RELATIONSHIPS CAN HURT FOR LIFE
GENERATION OF OFFENSE
JEALOUS SCAPEGOATISM
HEALTH IS *INDEPENDENT* MENTALITY
HEALING HARSH TRUTHS ABOUT PEOPLE
MY LIFE IN A GHOST TOWN
DUSTY FOUNDATION
PRIVACY! AN INALIENABLE RIGHT
HEAVEN IN A CELL
FINDING OUT WHAT IS NONSENSE
HUMAN SOCIETY IS CALUMNY
RESPECT A MAN WHO
CONSTANT INTERRUPTIONS OF LOSERS
STUCK IN LOWER DEVELOPMENT
THE EVIL STEPMOTHER SYNDROME
MUST DETACH TO BE HAPPY

AGING BABY

GETTING DUMPED CAN BE GOOD
IT'S ALL SOCIAL PSYCHOLOGY
EVIL DO-GOODERS
THINGS TO SAY/THINK UNDER ATTACK
PATHOLOGY ATTRACTED TO WOUNDED
LOSE BAD ATTRACTIONS
LET PEOPLE KNOW ABOUT THIS
SPLITTING
ESCAPE: GEOGRAPHICALLY RELOCATE
WAKE UP THEN NEVER THINK OF EM AGAIN
IT'S NOT HIM/HER BUT REPETITION COMPULSION
HOOKED TO MEAN CRAGGY FOOLS
BE YOUR OWN PARENT/ENCOURAGER
BIRDS, BEES AND STABILITY
FIDELITY IS ABOUT WHO *YOU* ARE
GO THRU A NARCISSIST TO KNOW HOW TO PICK
SATAN TAKES THE FORM OF CLIMATE CHANGE LEADERS
DEAD-BEAT FAR LEFT LEADERS
THOUGHTS ABOUT CURRENT POLITIX
I SUFFER FROM LACK OF ANIMAL FAT
STRINGENT DIETING OR DAILY FASTING
SKINNY HANDSOME COWBOYS EAT STEAK/PANCAKES
HOUSEHOLD THOUGHTS
PRUNE YOUR STUFF, NOW YOU CAN LOVE
JUST GIVE ME FRUIT, CHEESE AND NUTS
AN ONGOING WORK
YOU VS. THE FILTHY WORLD
DISCOVERIES TRIGGER INSIGHT
MATURITY IS INSULATION

AGING BABY

It really hurt getting involved with _________. It was like a black cloud or being eclipsed, it rattled my cage.

You will feel so much better healed from the narcissist--survivors say their whole life opens up after it.

He'll think and "create" from his ego mind and go awry, believe me. He's just a narcissist, you'll see.

Ghosting: You finally think you have someone to talk to but then it's obvious he's not there for you.

PRIMED FOR MADNESS

We're not asking China to change. We're just asking them to follow the rules. President Trump

From the boomers on, we've been primed for this: contagion of madness, mass lunacy.

When it becomes an out-of-control MASSIVE crowd filling cities it means war. Nothing else, prepare.

History shows armies of millions against millions. Massive crowds unseen before. It is WAR/must PREPARE.

MAYHEM unfolding in major cities cuz the liberal kiddies have been PRIMED for this since the 60's.

Out of control is something to GREATLY fear for people do in crowds what they'd NEVER do alone.

Twice as many whites are killed as blacks by cops. If they clear out the area's over-run by crime and rot.

Fine, the police will just evacuate your area and you'll have total crime. Blacks killing whites is ten to one.

It starts with vandalism and if left unchecked will quickly escalate into violence against all: **BEDLAM**.

They can't even arrest people--no chance--due to the sheer size of the dynamics/wanton violence.

Wisdom cries out in the streets. Proverbs 1: 20

Tho' I know it's causality the breakdown of society is still fascinating: Social Psychology.

Of course it's not Murder One, there'd be an acquittal and then it would be **REAL** thugish hell.

THRIVE THOUGH THEY HATE YOU

Let Trump be your exemplar: Tho' many hate him he doesn't care living the good life of a billionaire.

There are good people and bad. The bad people can repent and the good people can slip back.

God said stop butting heads in your thoughts. I got you away from all that, just enjoy what you've got.

Narcissists love to feed off an empath's pain. They seem them as ignorant/there's no need to explain.

He/she talks behind your back/does the smear campaign, repeating same cycle of being sweet then mean.

If you don't understand the dynamics of the narc tank you'll be cluelessly tossed to and fro drawing a blank.

If naive you'll be hit from all sides. God only knows where you'll end up--MUST get hip on these guys.

AGING BABY

This guy WANTS to hurt you--it's his daily meal--and he loves making you feel unworthy and jealous too.

The narcissist is THRILLED with your pain, he'll actually smile while saying "I'm so sorry for you man".

The entirely unique female let a bunch of boys in to her house and they nearly killed her for being odd.

WHY are narcissists so sadistic? Because they're pathologically envious of everyone, believe it.

Narcissism is everywhere in our selfish social generation which is entirely dumbed about our situation.

DIRTY OLD MEN [HIPPIES]

He talks too much about sex and I suspect he goes to prostitutes. Stay away from him/stay cute.

An old man like you talking about sex--man, get ahold of yourself! Get some decency, you can still excel.

An old man talking too much about sex--kick him outa your house as a DISGRACE. Return to the fifties, please.

A young man talking too much about sex--kick him out but teach him how he's been scammed by schools.

Shut the f--- up, you should be banned from youtube you sick old louse! Degrading people/instilling doubts.

Did you just say that to a 100,000 people? Are you kidding me? Get some class you hick, you're evil.

Shut the f--- up, you old hippie. You lost your morals before you even had any, a cultural tragedy.

DIRTY JOKES IN THE HOME

AGING BABY

Dirty jokes in a home are severe/immediate contamination of the psychic ambience creating new sinners.

No dirty jokes, **NO** off-color remarks, **NO** ogling of flesh, **COMPLETE** respect: give up on wanting this.

Shut up you old man talking about women's breasts. Ogling to your audience! You're a disgrace.

Disgusting! Telling the listener wives they should perform "BJ's" for their husbands---**BAN THIS MAN.**

What married couples do is not your business--keep your opinions to yourself old man, you're a disgrace.

But tech giants **WON'T** ban moral degraders--they want us immoral [for control] so they are high-rated.

JUST ASKING YOU GROW UP

All I'm asking is that you grow up finally. After all you're over a half century and should not be so silly.

So now all the wives who aren't giving "B-Js" will be the bad guys. How dare you, you old, **OLD** hippy!

So if a wife is too moral/comes from a Christian home or is old-fashioned [want you should want]--she's **BAD?**

To not sin requires strength: **RESTRAINT**--v.s. caving into devices to avoid anxiety cuz you're still weak.

No matter how flashy, charismatic, seemingly learned or wise--if not the right guy he'll cross your lines.

Narcissist is envious of everything--your other relationships, the fact you have feelings or think.

You're their friend just cuz they say you are--you can't choose. Then if you're not a friend they abuse.

You're losing yourself by valuing another too much. You've lost creative hunch and feel blah as such.

Raised to value self less than others, it happens easily so before losing yourself, catch yourself please.

If you have a tendency to lose yourself in relationship while placing too much value on the other, watch it.

With any deficit of worth and identity you will soak it up from another and lose yourself even more.

It's when your focus literally comes OUT of yourself onto another. Prior hobbies/interests lose their luster.

Breakup due to drinking but why was she drinking? Devaluation--what came first? chicken or egg

To officious questions just say "it's a long story best left to the anals of history" and they'll shut up, ok?

He's not perfect just assigned to me and that makes him perfect for me.

As narcissist inevitably creates chaos you lose yourself even more, waiting for the other shoe to drop.

NARCISSIST SH*T TESTS

As narc gives his shit tests and flip-flops of hot/cold the victim becomes tunnel-visioned and hypervigilant.

The shit tests are specifically purposed to see how much you can take. To find your limits he is testy and fake.

The victim becomes obsessed and addicted to the other. She loses her luster and is no longer clever.

She gives her truth away. Her "truth" is her focus, what she thinks about. Add love chemicals and her reality's out.

AGING BABY

What is love? The breaking down and merging of ego boundaries. Diminished even more, she's boring.

NARCISSISTS NEVER WANT CLOSURE

The narcissist never wants closure cuz he wants to keep up his supply—go no-contact and say goodbye.

The narc is so down-putting you feel a need for him to make you whole--a terrible place to be doll.

Going no-contact is about closing the energy: Isolating a tragedy and nipping it in the bud suddenly.

Because it's so easy to lurk we get hurt easy too and who needs this? Just your situation: IN SITU.

Just the thought of you makes me wanna cry. I felt that way around Jezebel once, it's the same spirit.

Someone who doesn't care about me but will build me up just to pop my bubble--was this not you too?

Years of addiction means years with that demon and he demands other actions just as deviant/bad.

The trick is to remember how they made you feel and never let em back, EVER. That's forever.

He's the kind who puts down women for face lifts but never for abortions. Again I say, avoid him.

It's the Little Digs that hurt the worst. They're happening constantly and it's our heart that hurts.

Why do narcs dislike those with boundaries? They can't. abuse one knowing her rights, surely.

The weak woman lets em in tho' mad at em. The strong says NO WAY/shuts the door without discussion.

AGING BABY

PROOF that feminism is pure B.S. and of no use to us: It aligns with Islam: total patriarchy/female abuse.

If your instincts say NO but you don't go along with it the result is emotional pain, disease and havoc.

WEAK WOMEN LET EM IN

When you're mad at yourself for not sticking to your NO the results are accidents, fatigue, thinking low.

It's our responsibility to back ourselves up. If we said NO we meant NO and there's no compromise sir.

Ranting about non-issues comes from low intelligence and you can't possibly bring him up lass.

Let him sink in his swill, as God gave him up you must also. Sin takes it's toll when people go low.

Let the empty thug go then a hole opens up and draws a new one FAR more appropriate for you luv.

When you're mad at yourself for not sticking to your NO the results are accidents, fatigue, thinking low.

Pull down the vain imaginations and idolizations of this faker and up your own fabulocity my dear.

Now's the time to dial it down about this guy. You've got different values and you introjected a lie.

You pasted your early trauma on him, infusing him with power as you longed for rejection torture.

Dial it down! Fight your idolization of this clown. You are fabulous and he's not even in the same realm.

De-idoloize him, he's not who you thought. You pasted the whole drama on him--stamp it all out!
CHARM ISN'T CHARCTER

AGING BABY

Stage presence and charm is not true character. Separate the two in mind and drop this lecher!

There are as many diets as there are human beings on earth. Rudolph Steiner

So that's how you know if someone loves you: they tell you no one likes you and treat you like trash.

Just say "NO! because you're nondiscerning and shallow--an embarrassment to anyone who knows."

God said I had to drop this creep outa my mind before He could do a NEW thing not so humiliating.

Evil is shallow and non-discerning. Is this not your neighbor, the church lady, just about everyone?

His last selection showed him to be COMPLETELY shallow and non-discerning, an embarrassment man.

He's a man who doesn't want to get old so acts like a told thinking it's cool and he's totally missing out.

Getting old is apex of life, art and talent: the highest Selfhood, achievement/style/crown of victory.

Go no contact, do it NOW! That means erasing him from mind--just work it on through and be DONE.

Remember, his shallow tolerance is evil! He wants to be seen as innocent but there's nothing he won't do.

One last shot or highest blend? A dinosaur ready to rot or the apex of a talent, the best God's got?

You reach a point of poetic pull power with your words and that's called mass appeal, how cool.

HE'S LIKE A SLOT MACHINE

AGING BABY

It's like a slot machine: maybe you'll hear maybe you won't. You want full time heaven not this rot.

Every time you break no-contact you get more obsessed and you still try to fix the problem--reject this.

Obsess/waste time over him, or spend that amount on your own situation? Being IN SITU is amazin'

I just want the quintessential. I don't want any superfluity or non-essentiality/assault on what you see.

CUED UP BY ORIGINAL TEMPLATES

If unloved as children we don't exist--dissociated from our own bodies--not centered within, but externally.

The sick relationships is where this dwindling self becomes second fiddle, an unmentionable, invisible.

Someone with a deficit of self and truth attracts an attention-whore, a hog--a sick combo without God.

They never return the attention and eventually use up the victims who will be discarded as the cycles end.

Once self is lost in another, the other's assessment of the victim is more important than her own: DANGER.

Self-focus may not feel normal after always giving yourself away but it keeps you from being nothing at all.

The narc sister said to the budding star: "You're not so great but the sad thing is you think you are".

If alone you're forced to evolve in more ways than those with a support system. Cut em loose, get strong.

Social people don't have to become better, stronger and smarter if always relying on someone to fixit sooner.

AGING BABY

It's not fair man: There's a breakup and one moves on and the other spends a decade in therapy or heroine.

30 years in therapy from being psychologically destroyed in a relationship from everything that annoyed.

Date long, marry slow and divorce fast cuz crazy doesn't show up for at least two years. George Bruno

He takes his man-cave wherever he goes but does he have to come into the she-shed and interrupt my show?

Women create order, men create chaos. I don't wanna believe this but every time he comes here I'm lost.

FOES DO THEMSELVES IN IF YOU DON'T

In liberal schools the conservative says "if I capitulate they'll be nice to me" but it never works, truly.

God's punishment may not come soon but when it comes it's a sudden smashing/I'd hate to be those goons.

I've been under God's wrath before--I've a healthy fear forever. Since that's the basis of wisdom, cheers!

Just cuz His sentence isn't executed speedily they assume they're free but then BAM: their greatest tragedy.

They get complacent cuz God didn't get em. That's how He draws em out--they get arrogant then are ruined.

First he went to prison, then he lost his teeth then just coasted until death-- that was your enemy.

First he was an arrogant kid who robbed me as supply. Next he was toothless on the streets, oh my.

People always underestimated me and that was always my secret weapon later with defeat of the enemy.

AGING BABY

Reward brilliance, ignore ignorance and punish rudeness. Geo Bruno.

EMOTIONS SPLINTER THE MIND

Bad relationships play with each others emotions to such a level that it fractures the mind, I was that kind.

They lower self-esteem to such a degree the thought of being alone they can't conceive: this is tyranny.

This isn't being melodramatic--it happens and it's the worst mind rape there is in this generation of sins.

Do you wanna marry me or do you just wanna be married? I love only you--feel like I always have--but won't hurry it.

Rejector is oblivious to pain he's caused/moves on while the other's head/heart is wrecked for years to come.

There are people traumatized for life from a bad relationship or parenting--brain grooves are unrelenting.

To fall so deeply in love only to have the rug pulled out is an unforgettable trauma affecting all of America..

LOW STRESS MARRIAGE: "HONEY"

End every sentence with "honey" then disappear into your own reality. Is that how marriage should be? It is for me.

They were perfectly normal before relationship but after they're a pathetic shell, I can attest to this.

Broken love bonds seek crutches feeling like love again then we wake up to a trash bin/it's over friend.

Before involvement realize there are PERMANENT psychological damages. A God given life, ravaged.

The more crazy you are in love the more you should question it, dove--is it the herd or from above?

AGING BABY

Love can be brutal. Lose your leg, get a prosthetic. A broken heart/lost love can last forever--think of that.

Many say leaving em alive with a broken heart/destroyed mind is worse than death--that's the great depth.

A mate can break you without you knowing it. A one-year relationship becomes ten years in therapy fixing it.

You can't love cuz you can't trust, have PTSD of course and depressed or anxious from the wrong person or worst.

Meanwhile the other person never thinks about you and doesn't care--this inequality of outcome isn't rare.

Knowing how much a bad influence can linger in consciousness for decades brings your restraint.

RELATIONSHIPS CAN HURT FOR LIFE

Weak men attract female aggression--not beating em up but constant bitchin', men are ALWAYS apologizin'.

Women are always saying men are better now, brought up by feminist moms/wives--not true, they're despised.

As indicated by their metacommunication your family doesn't want what's best for you but themselves.

What's best for you--success--makes them feel insecure, depressed and resentful, so you know the rest.

Most families are sick, it's normal. Most families contain the scapegoat syndrome, for example,

Just by spending the weekend with their family there's later a torrent of psychological poison flowing freely.

Be careful who you let into your mind and heart. It can be a thorn in your side for decades and REALLY hurt.

He loves invalidating--that's a new spin on it. It's not just a device he uses but something he glories in.

In this era, when someone leaves you they're most likely sleeping with someone else. Lush and louse!

GENERATION OF OFFENSE

This is the Generation of Offense. Everyone is supposed to apologize about everything even if innocent.

Now Trump is supposed to apologize about killing that terrorist? This is getting positively ridiculous.

In the last decade every man I met was apologizing to me. I asked "what for?" and they never knew, see?

Men are always apologizing cuz they've been groomed by feminist moms and wives cutting em down to size.

Men, stop apologizing. It's disgusting what's happened to western men and to our America it's crippling.

Feminist moms have wrecked their little boys. They even give em girl's toys and allow girls to punch/annoy.

JEALOUS SCAPEGOATISM

The family scapegoat may manifest the symptoms of all the others in the system--a walking lunatic asylum.

The scapegoat has no idea he's playing out the sick subconscious of the others but it's obvious he is.

It's like they pour in their judgements/psychoses together. He's a willing receptacle, the weakest member.

Envy: family doesn't want you to succeed. They want what is safest for you/them and what makes em feel better.

Can they stop scapegoating? No, cuz it's MOBBING: a group attacking one person purely for enjoyment.

What can the scapegoat do? Set boundaries, that's all--or he'll be hounded to death and very blue.

For happiness: We need to learn to live independently of the opinions of others: good, bad, whatever.

HEALTH IS *INDEPENDENT* MENTALITY

A good remedy is seeking OP-TRUTH: whatever they say, the opposite is the truth--this helps me too.

Don't hate your family, just don't look for consciousness where there is none. Richard Grannon

Start thinking like a psychotherapist, mechanically. Just think: there is no consciousness here, truly.

No consciousness just psychological darkness where the poop gets stuffed down and reprojected.

BUT what is repressed will eventually be expressed yet in another format, so watch out for the blowout.

To recover from the system, realize your problem is NORMAL but that you're not acting on your own.

It's those group TEMPLATES writing your scripts at times. It forms our perceptions, our self-understandings.

It's how Jane treated Mom and Mom treated Karen and how all of em gossiped about each other all day.

Realize they're only that way from bitterness that your life is better than there's or that's how they perceive it.

All they have is their perception. They don't know how tough it was working all day fearing destruction.

AGING BABY

They're jealous of the cars/the house or your status in life. They don't care what you went thru, the strife.

They're not gonna give up the map with secondary gains from maintaining status quo with them on top.

They don't **WANT** to start liking you cuz then they gotta deal with their own issues of always hating you.

They don't know a thing about society/politics just their own little world. It just slogans spouted by boys/girls.

To heal, do your own research on narcissistic personality disorder, projection, mobbing and scapegoating.

They mess you up, your mom and dad. They fill your head with thoughts they had and more, just for you. Old saying

HEALING HARSH TRUTHS ABOUT PEOPLE

These are harsh truths of what is normal but incredibly beneficial to you whenever you're blue.

I feel like I did when I was seven. I've cleared out all the bric-a-brac between now and then, I'm in heaven.

Of course, the victim being mobbed could be the perpetrator victimizing them with his sins.

Relationships may infect your with demons but if unaware you don't know it or why you look so unwholesome.

Relationships even casual can fill ya with the devil and you're unaware, not ever thinking of their evil.

All of a sudden you look haggard and old. You're being held down by something invisible, devilish, cold.

The recovered scapegoat still has huge feelings of guilt. We must go deep into the unconscious to quit it.

AGING BABY

Going deep connects you to the child and emotions. Now you're entire map can change/you'll start moving.

You wanna clean up your adult-neurosis to get to the child where every day is Saturday and it's happy/wild.

All these things like mobbings/scapegoatings are normal cuz man is born both sick/healthy, good/bad.

MY LIFE IN A GHOST TOWN

The past is trash and it's best not to look back. It's only your Ph.D. in the Streets and lessons in fact.

Mayberry was my favorite series. Everyone was happy but not married except for Otis who was drunk always.

It's not the END it's the beginning of the END and you're at your highest so don't put eldering down you ageist.

My ghost-town life of living with nothing provided a firm foundation cuz it was there I learned everything.

When I heard Old Borego was sold I cried. For tho' it seems like nothing it was where the old self died.

Ray had to wrench me outa my tiny cabin--I didn't want to leave for a mansion. Life is so strange isn't it?

It was a 1000 acres I was living on, in a ghost town. No car, rode a bike 6 miles for essentials--my happiest era.

I miss desert life, my strong foundation to go forward into the future. I think back and will never forget the era.

Living with nothing in a dusty cabin I was never bored nor lonely. When people came I asked em to leave me.

Sometimes friends would ask to hitch their trailer to stay. I said ok--then they'd ruin my privacy. BYE!

AGING BABY

I learned how social people were. They traveled in groups and would swoop in on me--I hated this for sure.

It was just like the old west, fraught with history. I was like the oldtimer at the door with a shotgun--go away!

DUSTY FOUNDATION

Now it's time to go forward to all God has for me, having learned from this unique/solitary/dusty history.

I had terrible problems and in desert solitude they all cleared up instantly. Dust off a mirror, happy.

I saw how happy I was without anything, didn't want anything and gave everything away. Main lesson, ok?

They'd ridicule me: What are you doin' in that dusty cabin? Then my eyes would go off to eternity and forget em.

In my new home I took only the quintessential items from the cabin and maintained my happy reclusion.

After being hounded by people, I was relieved when an oldtimer said "you can live you own life out there".

My OWN life: Without civilization's interruptions I really got into what that means--every minute so interesting!

I saw I could live in a cell and be happy. I had privacy, a free mind and a computer--that was total heaven to me.

PRIVACY! AN INALIENABLE RIGHT

Most importantly, PRIVACY. I could explore the inner rooms--mansions--in my mind, free of the unkind.

Even while writing this I can feel the spatiality, the vastness, the great meaning to me--I can return to it instantly.

AGING BABY

The 26 year experience was peppered with problems with the neighbors. Civilization again, all agitators.

Suddenly a bunch of people would come to the door. "Old friends" yah-right, it was this I abhorred.

The ghost town life was my boot camp, my Ph.D. in the Streets, the great humbler before moving forward.

It was so inspiring I was awestruck for all those years. Then in the new place out poured 106 books--so far.

Isn't God wonderful how He plans these things by pure miracle though at the time it seems unbearable?

Cabin life taught me what was quintessential--most essential--and in the new house I took only those few.

HEAVEN IN A CELL

Living in a cell would teach you the same thing--don't clutter up again I'm sayin', stay simple as zen.

Hoarders are the most unhappy people. A big house allows this evil as they hang on to the trivial.

Finding the quintessential in total order and simplicity was the greatest recovery over those who were fullabull.

Now in my big house I stay in the smallest room locked in. 80% of the rooms I rarely see except to clean em.

I don't see a big house and land as "living space" but the BUFFER ZONE between me and civilization.

Every time that jerk or Jezebel came it took months to heal, that's how sensitive you get--it's like an ordeal.

As ghost town's been sold and bulldozed for new owners I think it over and say: it's in me forever anyway.

AGING BABY

I'd walk into a dusty tin shed from 1910 and be **STRUCK** with the history when to others it was just junk.

The cabin itself was so shoddily made but that too was history and I was enthralled, totally fascinated.

Seeing so much in nothing was in itself the greatest education especially for a writer and thinker.

So I recommend to all, not European travel but a ghost town experience without folderol and nonsense.

FINDING OUT WHAT IS NONSENSE

Finding out what IS folderol/nonsense and the calibration of things that exist, and living my own life is total **BLISS**.

Now as I view the red mountains safe/warm/protected behind a wall, I think of a tiny cabin where I found God.

I had no relationship to bring me down/make me happy, I found that in privacy. Everyone's on probation with me.

After 26 years in total isolation in nature, I escaped the social devolution into debauchery, misery, censure.

Now I see how immature people are--they have totally regressed! Weird perversions and getting worse.

I matured in a tiny old dusty cabin. And now you're askin' me to go massive and it's also what God is sayin'.

My only company were cats, dogs, angels and God for 26 years in total desert solitude--it was my school.

Having missed 26 years in the evolution of our culture I'm not part of it anymore and shocked to my core.

At this stage of the game I'm so intricately set up and organized I can't have anyone around you guys.

AGING BABY

After total isolation for decades it's terrifying to be exposed suddenly but that I'm working on honey.

Isolation is my only comfy situation. To think of exposure--being out there--is overwhelming but I'm praying.

What a wonderful day it's been, ruminating about the past and all that I learned in the desert wilderness.

HUMAN SOCIETY IS CALUMNY

Horrors: My sister felt a perfect right to gossip and slander me to everyone even strangers. Calumny is soul murder.

She did it to her husband and made everyone hate him, to mom and to me but I mal-adapted as the weakest link.

I had no idea how my self-worth had crumbled, it was cuz she was gossiping, slandering, lying, mumbling.

I had no idea why my self-esteem was gone. It was from looking "up to" the herd not realizing it was wrong.

That's the way they have to be I guess, putting up with sisters ridiculing their visible incompleteness.

There are red flags in dating men/hexes: a man who hates his mom or speaks poorly about his exes.

When every single ex of his was crazy, had drama or it was her fault: watch out.

People who ARE drama carry drama wherever they go--now your life's in chaos and you don't even know.

If you're attracting the herd you could be the herd and that means weird and accepting all things, an evil curse.

Refusing to give in to a drive increases intelligence and will power. Just cuz you wanna hit 'er doesn't mean you should sir.

RESPECT A MAN WHO

Instead of being jealous when he speaks glowingly of exes, know what it indicates: he's to be respected.

Go for a man with class who respects his exes and has forgiven his mother so there's nothing unexpected.

Avoid men when your intuition says something is off or if you feel invaded with people when you're reclusive.

Before working things through with mom you're confronted by angry harridans: that's how it works ma'am.

If he's got anger issues with mom he's gonna repress it and later blow it out on you--and it's like a bomb.

Don't take on/succumb to modern diseases. They never took people before, it's how the social hypnotizes.

Addictions are devices to avoid anxiety in social situations, including mobbing/scapegoating in your systems.

I was dense to mom's abuse so when old harridans got like that I'd be blind to it but now I instantly intuit.

Forgive your mother--the maternal element, the bad mother template: now you'll have good fate.

Even if he's 95% perfect you sense something is off. That tiny bit's a siren calling for your attention, not to love.

Be SO careful who your friends are, your mates or who you're around--cuz their bad influence is profound!

Be careful who you give your heart to for it's a conduit to all the demons in em then decades are lost to mayhem.

The bad mother template was so entrenched in me it took decades to come back to true feelings and reality.

AGING BABY

As soon as I met a man I admired I'd feel jealousy and pick a fight cuz mom did that when higher than a kite.

All those experiences of total torture were so I could write em down in this ethology of human nature.

Having left a sheltered conservative home I was freaked out by liberal college and drank for courage.

It was shockingly disgusting to me and additionally they'd ridicule my Christianity. College was tyranny.

That's the ambience you wanna avoid in a man: social hypnotism, groupthink, social expectations.

When something seems off, better find out--cuz it always comes out later and then WATCH OUT.

CONSTANT INTERRUPTIONS OF LOSERS

If he doesn't know how to deal with drama he'll be constantly interrupted with crises and trauma.

That means he's constantly rescheduling, canceling or postponing dates. Watch this to avoid bad fate.

It's a red flag when he treats you nice but hates [dismissive/rude] on everyone else--could be you're next.

Major red flag: mood swings. Life of the party one day, super depressed the next. No way, move on Miss.

You want a rock in your life. Someone consistent and stable not a jovial party mood then filled with strife.

I figured since she gossiped so much about me to others she wouldn't mind me psychologically exposing her.

That's how women do things. That's how they take people out: gossip, slander, minimizing, starting rumors.

AGING BABY

Prepare for huge changes. You've come far from overcoming asses/finding Self whom God manages.

It was overwhelming--that's all I'm saying. But as God does things, I was buffered by being blind.

Only NOW--10, 20, 30 years later--do I see what happened cuz God knew I could when I finally awakened.

As you cut thru false matter/descend to your core you cry for days heavy with despair--then you're there.

Once you unhook your worth from that person walking out the door it's so much easier, for some it's all it took.

If you can't let go of an ex the chances of them being a narcissist and you co-dependent are near 100%.

STUCK IN LOWER DEVELOPMENT

In a Traumatic Childhood there is arrested development: it is STUCK at that stage then there's a SPLIT.

When stuck we split: He's either good or bad, black or white. The split manifests when walking away.

To make it easier to leave him she makes him into a demon but that's still stuck: truly let go, don't think of him.

She's trying to find her peace in that person walking out the door cuz that's what she's been imprinted for.

On the cognitive side you must unearth negative ideas about yourself--old grooves making life hell.

The codependent tends to project--thinking the other cares about them when they do not. Face it.

When stuck in early phases you must GRIEVE. As it comes to the surface you won't believe the tears, then RELIEF.

AGING BABY

He with a pathological need to feel superior will trigger your earlier less-than schema you had with others.

I felt inferior, ashamed, less-than and codependent after hearing him talk but then I was ok when I got back.

I thought: Maybe I don't know how to cook, to dress, to decorate and insecure feelings brought bad fate.

And it's all because they put you in a trance after creating the illusion they know everything. Baffling!

THE EVIL STEPMOTHER SYNDROME

First you marry the wrong man, then you're brought down by his kids then you're hated cuza what they did.

It spreads out in concentric circles, man. These ancillary relations just cuz you got hitched/yoked to him.

Cuz when his act is over and the real barbarian comes out, watch out. The ontologically fatal insight: ouch!

The Evil Stepmother Syndrome is hateful. He could kill you, or his kids could kill you, so be careful.

His kids hate your guts cuz you're not mom so if you start acting out watch out you're now their scapegoat.

It was just a brief thing, a passing fancy, a template trigger, magnetism, someone I thought I knew but hell no.

But if you got HOOKED to him, oh man now the fun starts as you're minimized, demeaned, used and blocked.

You say what should be written on twitter and what I should not: according to who, you? Where is this rule.

Though we're alike in many ways I now see how we're opposites and sorry it's too much to pay.

That's how Satan gets ya: 99% right and 1% deadly wrong. There's some truth to all things but it's not God.

I saw you in one way then I saw you in another. So sorry I can't return to the other but that's life brother.

With the Solitude Solution you're all on probation. I'm invulnerable to the rabble at a very high station.

He's not perfect but he's perfect for me if he brings me stability. That's the function of a man, truly.

I'm sorry but I don't see you as I did--I just don't, kid.

Life has enough problems without mood swings of high then low--you need him to weather your storms.

Sometimes the only answer is to detach from the family. There's too much mess there, it's beyond mending.

Many members may need therapy and they won't take it from you, so be wise and just let it go.

In a system used to it, they need you to stay a grasshopper in a pit. It doesn't matter what you do to change this.

They're deeply invested in keeping you down in the mud. So what can you do but detach and go forward.

MUST DETACH TO BE HAPPY

Always find a way to detach from the opinions of others--but it's not always complete due to tribal filters.

If you encounter mobbing/scapegoating/bullying remember you aren't who they say you are, and go on.

The systems approach is a very scientific way of seeing reality and can completely change your identity.

AGING BABY

They wanted you down in the bad identity. You were a grasshopper because they needed you to be.

The detached zen approach would be just to observe: he's abusing me and I feel depressed, I've lost my nerve.

Buddha: All of life is suffering, suffering comes from attachment, the end of suffering is detachment.

How do you detach? You get off the hook by clean living and intentions--now they have no influence.

RECAP: Clean up your act and you're off the hook, the hook being attachment [distress, trauma, threats].

Another way of saying this is: if you feel shame [from addictions etc] others can control you, that's it.

Addiction, attachment ruining the day: I say something and you're triggered into feeling a certain way.

Part of the guilt/anger/rage is that you don't fight back. You're gonna have to set boundaries and do that.

Fighting in the corner means asserting your boundaries when they're triggering you--it's a milestone too.

Either assert your boundaries or get out. The former brings more attacks, the latter brings clout.

GETTING DUMPED CAN BE GOOD

Getting dumped can be good cuz now you don't have to put up with em anymore. Think only of that dear.

Now you don't have to tolerate crap, they're someone else's problem: that's how to see your dumping.

See it as a wine test: You tasted it then spit it right out. Now someone else can taste/feel the drought.

AGING BABY

I feel so much better after letting you go. The delirium of up and down is gone and I'm gettin' ready to show.

You say you're positive but all you do is critique from your viewpoint which in itself is assuming a superior take.

All I hear from you is criticism and gaslighting while assuming the dominant view, the old school.

My sister called me ugly at age ten and I never got over it. See, I'm a psychologist.

Don't EVER make excuses for who you are with. That is the most demeaning thing I have ever heard of.

IT'S ALL SOCIAL PSYCHOLOGY

It's social psychology: the masses are whimsical, fickle, easily steered by evil, unpredictable--the rabble.

I can hear people yelling at me. Stop it I say--this internal dialogue has gotta go to get ready for creativity.

I'm sorry, you just reminded me of someone I thought I knew. Just a passing fancy or a template too.

Falling in love with your youtube psychology mentors is one way of substituting templates/intentional or not.

Someone you REALLY admire who is helping you. God takes it so far but with a fork in the road, bid adieu.

You think of the stuff he is saying and it erases crap or massively/completely explains it--it is relieving.

A massive youtube following is one way to get approval where there was none but thru degrading em?

DON'T tell em to have sex as a prelude to friendship--that is ridiculous! Get some class, this is serious.

Don't look back/down just be grateful something FAR worse didn't happen. You just needed the lesson.

You've gotta close that door on the narcissist so you can heal. Going no contact is the only way with heels.

You must have empathy to understand narcissist abuse, or why going no-contact is so essential for a muse.

If he says there is no narcissist he knows nothing of pathology of psychopathy or he's without empathy.

EVIL DO-GOODERS

The do-gooder who denies a teen's narcissism has never heard of it and says to let him in, no big thing.

Narcissism is about a lot more than "he likes himself a little too much" or "he's just loves himself a bunch".

One frenemy enabler was a Baptist lady who insisted I let em in. This lady was a most dangerous "friend".

LET EM ALL IN: That's the mantra of the evil do-gooders who forgive everyone though still fullasin.

LET EM ALL IN: even juvenile delinquents or cultures who hate us/who rape women in immodest dress.

Social Culture since WWII is the most dangerous of all. For DISCERNMENT is totally gone, they're all good ya know.

You can't get anywhere tangling with a narc. You wanna be ready for sweet people and to have an open heart.

Part of your healing is wondering why you let him into your life in the first place--what red flags were missed?

We stay connected to a narcissist due to inner wounds from a narcissist in our past--denial lasts.

AGING BABY

If you don't heal the trauma bond, you won't be able to let go of this bum. Heal first to block the scum.

I had to close the door on my castle and not let any of em in cuz they sought only to take and cause hassle.

After a painful divorce and family mobbing I splashed into the desert and was instantly invaded with same.

It's true that if still unhealed, the attachment trauma is still there begging to be reconnected--even with them.

THINGS TO SAY/THINK UNDER ATTACK

I can't be around you cuz I admired you so gulped down your devaluation which stopped the writing again.

I don't care what you think cuz your thoughts are rinky-dink, same old school false narrative, a stink.

That's what I do, and I trust what I do without explanation, so your critiques/devaluations are ignored man.

Why upon meeting you did I suddenly lose confidence? I recall those years seeking social acceptance.

There's something about him that puts you one-down. Can't locate it but go silent when he's around.

You can remain superior while being feminine and ladylike. You can put him in his place without words/strife.

Listen lady: Take time to heal, heal, heal. You'll be armored by getting to know yourself as God's child.

For if you're **NOT** healed you let crud in again and again. You'll feel desperate for connection--with anyone.

The victim must heal her "frozen feelings"--the jumble of mal-adaptations and abuse making her obtuse.

You must heal the template causing your attraction to harmful people. No-contact does that/blocks evil.

Of all diseases and maladies, attachments to people bring the most devastation and death without cease.

We are social animals I hear, social hypnotism reigns: the acculturation process, or bell-shaped curve.

How can we possibly heal being around someone who is harming us? Why let him in to do it again?

Stop saying it's an autobio--of course it is with any female psychologist and that doesn't debunk it narcissist.

PATHOLOGY ATTRACTED TO WOUNDED

Pathological people attracted to the wounded. That's their whole process to exploit/get supply/be supported.

If you can't let go of an abusive person [trauma bonded] you are prey for this guy again, unable to say No.

Shane retraumatized me over and again cuz there was never any healing of original trauma with you mom.

What makes men think that the actual experience of these things is illigit but mere book knowledge is?

To go No Contact, say: I am worth it, I am worthy, I don't deserve this, there's more out there for me.

Spend all time bringing the energy back into yourself and your HOME. That's where it's all at for a woman.

I filled my home with colored lights and interesting niches. This is my domain free of jerks, Jezebels and witches.

Now you're alone begin seeking healthy relationships and setting boundaries to divert any more tragedies.

AGING BABY

The guru advising sex as a prelude to friendship--does that mean he's slept with every female friend he has?

If you gotta deal with the narc you go Grey Wall or Low Contact, get that? It's still you free from hell.

I needed to grow up inside, do my inner child work, heal my emotions, get back my feelings: "I don't want you here".

I was imposed on/invalidated so much I wrote 106 books on it. It's like a torrent and so ultra-complicated.

LOSE BAD ATTRACTIONS

I'm no longer attracted to people abusing me, using me, triangulating me, using flying monkeys against me.

NO MORE: pulling you into drama triangles, making you feel chaotic, taking you off your path. Jenna Ryan

Tell kids political correctness is a means to control speech and not to call anyone a hater/bigot with a breech.

We should all feel sick of political correctness--we should hate it as a cancer eating at the soul of a country.

As you gain clarity thru whatever means he'll go to the periphery outa the center. Now you're there.

They're not educated but brainwashed. They can't discern differences, they can't do their own research.

Debate's a great thing. But not with political correctness--it is their way or the highway/they get violent even.

Let em know war's a racket. Smidley Butler

Most people have no heart nor soul. They want what they want and couldn't care less about the high toll.

Let me be candid: don't trust people.

AGING BABY

If they know when your husband's funeral is they'll break in then and take everything you own: don't trust people.

LET PEOPLE KNOW ABOUT THIS

Make em know they are controlled by an industry which promotes Satanism/pedophilia/murder.

Tell em porn is an evil Satanic tool to make em normalize perversion/debauchery/sodomy.

Porn is there to degrade and objectify women while making men weak and destroying the family/blurring lines.

If it doesn't make sense, someone's makin' money. Old Adage

One way to look at getting dumped is: You are now free. If they went to another, they're not--see?

When dumped you didn't lose, you won. They weren't valuable, stop thinking they were: it's freedom.

All relationships are utilitarian--we're getting things from them--it's how they treat you after they get em.

They come to you for the thing they want then they go away. They're using you and it's hell to pay.

The reciprocation isn't there, or a general lack of concern for you. They come and they go, you're blue.

SPLITTING

Narcissist mom sets a unique set of circumstances--e.g. splitting the Golden Child from the Black Sheep.

Splitting: I remember it vividly. No matter what I did to change it the split remained: her good/me bad.

Golden Child is selected for special treatment as his/her bad deeds are covered up/reframed as positive.

AGING BABY

Every good deed is magnified/brought to attention while the black sheep tho' achieved is never mentioned.

For the black sheep, even a charitable deed will be reframed as something mean and nasty.

Hard times create strong men creating good times creating weak men creating hard times. Geo Bruno

ESCAPE: GEOGRAPHICALLY RELOCATE

You can go from hatred to love just by geographically relocating: overnight all social clots dissolving.

In a psychological sense, the word narcissist implies the need to abuse--it implies sadism, no small thing.

Like a fair fun-house, the narc is fine seeing the distorted mirror cuz you help keep it alive. If you don't, die.

Anyone questioning this illusion will be attacked aggressively for that's what they're for, really.

If you attack their false identity the level of vociferousness and viciousness will shock you, I've seen this.

Gotta go no-contact so you can heal. Move him mentally to the periphery then come center/start to feel.

WAKE UP THEN NEVER THINK OF EM AGAIN

One benefit of waking up to the narcissist is not wanting to even think of em again and not caring again.

When you build a narcissist up they don't build you up, but spread it around to others. You end up losing for it.

Because when you build up a narcissist it does not come back to you. They start taking you down too.

Narcissist uses the new growth from you to get better supply and move up the chain, that's the game.

That is the antithesis of a relationship. Status-climbing no love-bonding but it's basic to the narcissist.

The narcissist steals your stuff/flaunts it in your face while subtly devaluing you and you feel like dirt, the Ace.

You may feel very low energy after all this but INSTEAD feel free of them for you've been drained in an illusion.

I gave him everything and after he took all that I was exhausted. That is the experience with any narcissist.

Narcissists go no-contact, give you the silent treatment or ghost you, but they always come back.

It's not Jack or Joe whom you need but an unmet need which should have been filled long ago.

The only way to eradicate this syndrome is to recognize and meet that unmet need on your own.

IT'S NOT HIM/HER BUT REPETITION COMPULSION

It's not the guy or gal but repetition compulsion from the big gaping holes inside demanding you fill em.

Unless you go in and do the work yourself you're gonna be stuck forever in repeat. See solitude as neat!

You wanna get to the point of non-attraction and being put off by narcissist types who idolize then split.

It's the idolization phase that snags you but the devaluation phase [only for love addicts] hooks you.

It's a painful truth but an incredible revealing and health-giving one. It's not him or her, they're nothing.

HOOKED TO MEAN CRAGGY FOOLS

To encapsulate it in four words: you're hooked to meanness.

Work on unmet need within or always be chasing after em. It's not him, on close observation he's craggy-lookin'.

You're hooked to meanness even by the craggy-lookin' cuz your mode is set to CORRECTION of past or present.

We don't feel like we're ever enough if there were unmet needs when young-- that's how we're programmed.

How we are programmed: Seeking affirmation from people who are unable to give it--that's the repetition.

Brain tries to get it right with mom decades back: by making someone love me today who won't in fact.

If caught in this syndrome you'll be very good at picking the ones who don't/can't love you hon'.

If caught in this syndrome you'll be good at picking those who can't love you hon'--the cycle's never done.

The only time to get those needs met was in childhood--externally met by parenthood--but now you should.

That was the only time to get it done externally and if not you must GO BACK and do it yourself, truly.

BE YOUR OWN PARENT/ENCOURAGER

Be your own parent and encourager. That's loving yourself and the child within while rejecting him or her.

He's reached his peak now watch his decline as he does himself in. You've taken enough/he's in declension.

Usually when we can't let go of someone it means he's totally not good for us- -everything's in opposites.

AGING BABY

It's the way he stole your stuff while minimizing you too. Narcissist contradictions are a frustrating stew.

Going no-contact is not hurtful but huge release. The thing you avoided brings you to center, pleased.

Ask yourself: WHY am I loving this person and has this happened before where I can never get him?

Always look at patterns to get any answer. If things repeat themselves there's a wealth of info for sure.

The person walking out the door with you pining over them indicates one thing: your parents, the same sting.

It's a lot deeper than you think. It's not 1-2-3 here's how you let go, no matter how nondescript/rinkydink.

Coming through that big black cloud I learned there is NOTHING that controls me but the Holy Spirit.

And I'm no longer controlled by some old template bringing attractions to indifferent mates who are third-rate.

BIRDS, BEES AND STABILITY

Men and women are made for each other, that's just nature. It's the birds and the bees/what fits sir.

Always talking about beautiful women triggering attachment trauma/making himself up over ya?

All I want is stability in a mate. Not up one day, down the next but every day the same as we CELEBRATE!

Marriage is where every meal's a banquet and every day's a celebration and that's called a happy home.

Not this crap of you playing games and me being tied in through past templates--that's childish, forget it.

AGING BABY

So your mom was indifferent and your dad was drunk. Face it then move forward without all this junk.

When you're still mad as hell but behind a wall that's PTSD which brings memories up like you're there now.

You're not hanging on to a man nor a woman. This is hanging on to something you never got man.

It's something you vitally need in your soul and thus the pedestal and inability to let go.

THIN: I have to be. Things just don't work right unless I'm like a jockey. Eating once daily it's easy.

There were several eras in the desert, each one less entrenched: less people/freer/happier/relaxed.

FIDELITY IS ABOUT WHO *YOU* ARE

You stay with your mate not because of who they are but because of who YOU are. Fidelity marks the star.

God has commanded wives to love their husbands [whether they do or NOT] so you've got to ma'am.

You can work things out cuz you loved each other at one time. Work on self, then he will, then begin again.

If you love him [even tho' you don't] and treat him lovingly he'll respond in kind then things are friendly.

All anyone wants is love anyway, to have a happy home like they did or didn't in the day and to have tranquility.

You've got kids to bring up and pets to take care of. The trash taken out, the lawn mowed, it's never enough.

For the home to run like a Swiss watch you gotta work as a synchronous bunch. That's a home, like a corporation.

AGING BABY

I don't care if you watch TV just mow the lawn and take the trash as you said you would, now you're free.

Marriage is where every meal's a banquet and every day's a holiday and God wants it for you, ok?

Even if he's in another part of the house and you never see him it's still a home--you can still be alone.

There's an order and you're only happy if you follow it. God over man, man over woman, woman over children.

When women did male chores and men did women's chores nothing got done any good anymore.

GO THRU A NARCISSIST TO KNOW HOW TO PICK

To find the right one you gotta go thru the narcissists. This builds appreciation for the right kind of fish.

There are two kinds of people, the humble and those who are about to be. Anonymous

The inner work to change the template of bad attractions is new neuropathways. New grooves--not the old ways.

Before these neuropathways--old templates from history--are changed we'll choose the guy who hates me.

The one that doesn't want you feels right because as a child you were imprinted towards a rejecting kind.

Like a baby duck following it's mother you're following rejection and are revolted by the nice guy hon'

If Paul used "I" 24 times in ten verses why can't I say "I"? Please tell me why.

Ok, I went through it but I'm also an expert in it. Why are there all these divisions--in psychology?

You can't get over him if you're idolizing him. It's freedom from pain knowing these things.

SATAN TAKES THE FORM OF CLIMATE CHANGE LEADERS

Satan takes the form of a climate change political leader or a politician or a socialist giving away everything.

Our wonderful life-saving alpha male president believes "weakness is provocative"--that sounds so good.

Kalergi Plan: To make us all-brown and genocide us whites who are blamed for everything since time began.

Mexico: 60,000 people missing since 2006, only 1000 between '64-to then. Can you even imagine?

At that time slavery was worldwide. It's the white man who freed the slaves in a civil war where 600,000 died.

Trump's not starting a war he's restoring effective deterrence. That's how it's done you dunces.

Blame Obama for the missiles shot by Iran. This traitor of America paid em billions that bought em.

If they didn't control speech on social media it would naturally move to the right.

President Trump doesn't want war but he's not gonna just look the other way when Americans are killed, ok?

DEAD-BEAT FAR LEFT LEADERS

AOC--"deadbeat Cortez"--is just a far-left narrative and the democrats are becoming fed up with her.

AOC riles dems cuz she won't pay party dues. It's the left eating itself: irresponsibility/entitlement, refusal.

AGING BABY

What has Pelosi done for the American people? Turn over the House to the radical left, upstarts and rabble?

Pelosi and goon squad are trying to reshape this country into a socialist agenda and we're sick of all of ya'.

Pelosi made a huge mistake trying to appease her radical left youth base. A strategic error from a lifted face.

THOUGHTS ABOUT CURRENT POLITIX

Though white people built this country they are the most hated group like the South African tragedy.

We owe it to the millions of murdered souls to hear stories about the holocaust and to never stop.

Those who make peaceful revolution impossible make violent revolution inevitable. John F. Kennedy

Hah: In typical liberal female fashion, Pelosi's trying to appease the liberal base while saving face.

AOC's a typical socialist: the "pay your fair share" mantra and "wealth distribution" only applies to others.

Liberal Merkel and Harry are coming under the protective nurturing arm of Obama and Oprah--predictable.

This really is a blight on the monarchy if it's a left wing thing that makes em billions, think of it.

Why is it after thousands of years of teaching two genders they can now take your kids if you dare think it?

Tell kids actors/musicians they adore/model after are not real people but manufactured fronts for globalist evil.

All races are totally different don't tell me they aren't--and for them to be humane they must have higher IQ.

AGING BABY

Telling people to look up crime stats by race isn't racist. Blacks killing blacks is what is shows: face it.

They come here hating white people and America. Go away you traitors after we've been so kind to ya.

Decriminalizing theft [even murder]: every shop is robbed every hour and nothing can be done: we're OVER.

ACLU putting tampon machines in men's bathrooms is an overthrow of reality--they want us crazy.

Pelosi: does being good mean no retaliation? We gotta establish good deterrents! Stupid woman retire.

Trump is the president of there-will-be-consequences-for-killing-Americans and that's why we love him.

I SUFFER FROM LACK OF ANIMAL FAT

I suffer from lack of cheese and butter. If I swerve too much to the starch skin gets a little like leather.

I suffer from lack of pizza. Gotta have it every single day--extra cheese please.

If I look young for my age it's from two things: eating once a day and being alone: no [SS] Status Stress.

I have to keep remembering that the most important work is not working. Music/colored lights are helping.

It is SO fruitful to not-work, to go into diffuse perceptual mode outa tunnel vision. Party time, all day long.

I filled the house with strobe lights and different musical areas and it's a fantastical homestead so rare.

Mystery, beauty, color, thought, peace, tranquility, eternity, intelligence, creativity, elemental reality.

AGING BABY

I guess I'm a housebound anti-social creep. This is my highest apex because in solitude I'm at my peak.

You look in the mirror and see signs of wear and tear, years and tears. So what, you're saved by the experts.

The traumas you go through growing up/maturing show on the face but it can be refined to show you as the Ace.

Old age is NOT the end, its your highest blend. You're at the top of your game so age is your friend.

What a noisy house. Kitten hockey with a stone inside, dog tennis in the afternoons, entertainment they love.

Ageist ridicule is terrible. Famous females may not even need facelifts but anything to shut up the rabble.

STRINGENT DIETING OR DAILY FASTING

As a Daily Fastarian I eat HIGH fat and HIGH carb together and weigh far less than any dieter.

The plastic surgeon said I didn't need a facelift. At my age how could this be? Cuz I fast every day, see?

Don't feel right about buying a hundred steaks/freezing em for my daily mealers for there's two kinds of eaters.

The carnivore diet heals, I'm sure it does. There are eyebags tho', indicating kidney--just cover it up.

It works at first then the kidneys start to clog. It shows in the face--you looked younger before, ok?

2018 summer you looked younger. Why is that? It's before your crazy dieting which works at first then danger.

They warn against high fat combined with high carb but that's the American breakfast fueling our work.

AGING BABY

All breakfasts across the world are high carb and high fat or protein. Who restricts? The crazy Americans.

Especially if your buying your steaks at Walmart. You're gonna have eyebags soon but go ahead, enjoy it.

Every day dad ate bread, lotsa butter, bacon and eggs. He died at 85 with black hair and flawless face.

The beautiful Europeans have bakery for breakfast. Rolls and croissants with lotsa butter, think of it.

Is it necessary that we stuff all these vitamins in the meat, or just carb-up with glucose as we used to think?

Where MacDougal [Starch Solution] went wrong is his deletion of FAT. Eat starch/fat together like your dad.

But then they don't eat again. They don't have candies in the afternoon unless the healthy ones by Karen.

You look good, you eat only beef. But you looked far better before and that's something for you to explore.

SKINNY HANDSOME COWBOYS EAT STEAK/PANCAKES

Skinny good-lookin' cowboys had pancakes, eggs, bacon and usually didn't eat again--Daily Fastarians.

You actually think a skinny goodlookin' cowboy craves lettuce? No, when he eats it's most calorically DENSE.

What's more efficient: eating starch three times a day [MacDougal] or starch-and-fat once a day, fool?

To me eggs taste campy/like a sewer and bacon too, not my lure but BUTTER and CHEESE: that's for me.

There are whole European cultures into dairy exclusively to not have deficiencies from not eating meat.

AGING BABY

Depletion's a terrible thing. You can get so depleted you can't walk and breathe at the same time. Get healthy

That's my present take on diet. I realize I've cycled through all of em so all I can do is express the current.

From coffee I get acid-reflux all day but 1/2 caffeine pill works great. Many things we learn along the way.

When I saw him again I couldn't believe how he'd aged. It was that crazy diet, and here he was a sage.

Yes, potatoes are nightshades and we shouldn't eat em but I was brought up on em as a Scotch woman.

HOUSEHOLD THOUGHTS

Homesounds: crows, aft breeze in trees, crickets at night, wind chimes, bells, birds, light tunes throughout.

There's no greater habit than getting up at midnight. When they're asleep, wow--I'm productive/high as a kite.

My dogs and cats beg for Karen's Healthy Candies. Figs, raisins, dates, nuts, coconut, cacao, nutbutters.

Music is never a waste of time. It is totally inspiring. Music first THEN work to make it bulls-eye hitting.

I don't have time for this, I got projects: clean house, feed pets, cat hockey, dog tennis, music, cat naps.

I stopped dieting but when it was time to lose weight God pruned me down to 98--agile, elastic light freight.

As much as I love old cowboy movies nothing compares to music and I always see that's where I should be.

I expect the household to run like a Swiss watch, a corporation, a library and a monastery.

AGING BABY

As **NEAT** as a hotel, as fascinating as a strobe light bar and as quiet as a monastery when I want it.

For the home to run like a Swiss watch you gotta work as a synchronous bunch. That's home, **ORDER** and love.

How to order and simplify your house: Put everything you aren't using in the basement/empty it every so often.

Have a Basement Sale: Call all the neighbors to come take it for free if they will haul it away/get ready for new.

I want **ORDER!** If I don't have order or if there is chaos I'm not a happy momma--dirty disorder is hell on earth.

Use basement as your recycle bin—the stuff isn't gone, don't panic. You just don't use it and will forget it.

Then when the time comes to make way for new, out it goes--call a basement sale for your good stuff.

I'm constantly ordering my stuff. That's a female thing: sorting socks, just the quintessential/hoarding sux.

PRUNE YOUR STUFF, NOW YOU CAN LOVE

I can't count up the stuff I've given away just to make way, streamline, hone down, simplify, clarify, get happy.

Don't hold on to any superfluity/non-essential. Be ready to go in a minute: everything in a duffle for example.

I wanna know just what **ARE** those essentials—so that in an emergency I'm prepared and just take those.

Going with fly by night attractions brings instability to the household. It's an undercurrent, deceptive/cold.

One meal is heaven and necessary. Two meals is acid reflux and choking at night so I fast all day.

AGING BABY

I eat HIGH fat [butter/cheese] and HIGH carb [pizza, noodles, potatoes] and couldn't be healthier.

If you wanna eat only animals, go ahead but I couldn't. It satiates but some can't bear it/it's not Americana.

The handsome/pretty/skinny Americans decades back had pancakes/butter/syrup/bacon/eggs for breakfast, ok?

Stop your silly dieting/food restricting and just eat whatever you want once a day, then fast/be happy.

My home made pizza is high-fat and just enough thin-crust carb. It satiates for the day so I can soar.

Let no one impose their dead diet dogma on you. There's millions of diets, we're omnivores, enjoy it.

This is the conclusion I've reached after decades of dieting and food dogma: Eat like they did in history.

By far the most productive past time is music looking out the window to the red mountains surrounding me.

Forget thin crust pizza and low carb. I love my fluffy crust and I add lotsa butter to satisfy all day long.

JUST GIVE ME FRUIT, CHEESE AND NUTS

Just give me some fruit, cheese, a few nuts. That's why I store that stuff in our new freezers for snacks.

Your looks will tell you when it's time to reverse. Things get lumpy and pasty and you feel worse.

Too many mornings of cinnamon rolls with butter in a row, time to reverse into shrimp/salmon for awhile.

The sins are usually food, sex and drugs. I used to be a food sinner but now I never think of grub.

AGING BABY

Vaccines are bioweapons. They are meant to destroy you and harm your biology/your brain [make you crazy].

I'll always be anorexogenic since I prefer thinness like a Jockey, low-weight lives longer and feels better.

I'll always be anorexogenic the way I prefer isolation and shun all groups-- except my own, that's the scoop.

Mayberry was my favorite series. Everyone was happy but not married except for Otis who was drunk always.

It's not like South Korea where everyone has facelifts and it's totally scientific. There are botched jobs, tragic.

If chemically sensitive I'd think it safer to have a facelift than all those chemicals shot in under the skin.

Botox can be dangerous--it's really still just an experiment.

AN ONGOING WORK

It flows all day from midnight on. I see it as destiny cuz it comes out automatically despite only 4 hrs sleep daily.

You have a goal, ya know. To get to that goal you just do anything you must, you grin and bear it or bust.

It's an ongoing work--I'm not gonna rush completion of any part of it. Let it sit, ruminate my uncle insisted.

I'm ready to publish Aging Babies but think I'll put it on simmer for awhile since I'm so much a part of it.

Baby boomers are from 1946-1964 so everyone within that range are your peers with whom you have rapport.

Is musing while looking out the window a trivial pursuit? No, it's the most superior time use.

In the desert wilderness for thirty years I was a sitting duck without a car or a fence. I had to learn defense.

While it was very difficult being alone in the desert I developed in different ways from the others.

YOU VS. THE FILTHY WORLD

Your mentors should be money/wealth, fitness/health and navigating relationships. George Bruno

A pattern of greatness is separating from the family system then when whole coming back to re-ignite them.

Stop remorsing over those eras when the devil had control. Anything can happen then but now you are whole.

You weren't yourself. Remember that and from now on be strong because Satan takes over weak vessels.

Be a psychological engineer: Why are they acting like this? Cuz it's enjoyable to feel superior in a group-dis.

Gluttony and perversion goes together all through history and cheating is cheating--there's always treachery.

In states where there's most porn there's most plastic surgery as wives compete with teen wanna bes.

Pushing the envelope is pushing down culture. Making perversion cute like Blanche in the Golden Girls.

Women perverted after Blanche in the Golden Girls. Sluts are Cute was the message so they gave it a whirl.

DISCOVERIES TRIGGER INSIGHT

In discoveries you don't tell em what to think. You trigger their unconscious analogies, bringing INSIGHT.

AGING BABY

Of **COURSE** it's attraction. If you wanna be a success, make yourself apt for success first, this is obvious.

It's not "attraction" in a law of affinity metaphysical sense, but finding yourself by removing the superfluous.

It's what I do. It's what I was born to do, after having eliminated the shrew obstructing the muse.

Neurotic: Wanna be rich and famous. Healthy: wanna make a serious/amazing new dent [fabulous].

Life phases: You know you have limited time left, the end of your journey--so you don't put up with crazy.

Everything preceding Old Borego was simply horrible cuz it involved people but for my books great raw material.

30 years ago sister ridiculed cuz books weren't finished. Did she think it could all be done in a minute?

Books weren't written until theory was established and pure--not books written before I had matured.

Am I mature now? Yes for it means insulation. I'm safe and separate in my own home--crucial for a woman.

Not running around all day to this and that but staying home cuz nothing out there is as interesting: fact.

MATURITY IS INSULATION

People aren't into life-long projects [greatness] but many projects quickly finished [stale, shallow, aimless].

Fork in the road: opportunity/change or old dramas and chaos. Most choose chaos, programmed by asses.

When things don't make sense: Hang in there, create a new normal, wait for storm to pass. Geo Bruno

AGING BABY

Most people are impatient and hate the idea of waiting. But it's entirely true: when in doubt do nothing.

I don't wanna read you longwinded readup to the point. Spit it out--START with what you're talking about.

If you're great/profound they could walk you by--that's how it always is in dense generations under the sky.

It's about ready to bust wide open after years of working underground but still God's timing is profound.

It's a bit frightening after being isolated for 30+ years like solitary confinement in my own self-imposed monastery.

God said you'd no more be hidden under a bushel so I'd say you'd better get ready for the time is late lady.

It was forty years of a slow, laborious, painful path but God gave me many respites. This isn't overnight sis.

It's been gradual for forty years, ok? Slow and steady, a writer from midnight on every single day.

When God stops talking to you it gets dark doesn't it? When that fellowship is broken with the lord, death.

100 KAREN KELLOCK BOOKS

AFFINITY OR MISERY
AGELESS CORNUCOPIA
AMERICA AWAKE!
AMERICA'S DAFT ERA
ARTS OF PALEO FASTING
AUTOPHAGY ON CHEATERS
BACKSTABBING NEUROTICS
BETRAYAL TRAUMA
BOOMERS AND BROKENNESS
BOOT ON NECK
CHAMPION GUIDES
COMMIE NUTHOUSE
COMMIES
COMMUNIST SPIRIT
CONTAGION OF MADNESS
CONTAGIOUS MADNESS
CULTURE CLASH BASHED
DAFT LEFT
DAILY FASTARIAN
DAM RATS
DIVERSITY IS CRUELTY
E-RACE WHITE
EVIL FREAKS (Beyond Gross)
THE END OR A BEND?
FEMALE BULLIES AND FEMI-NAZIS
FEMALE CARNALITY
FEMALE DUMB DOWN
FEMALE POWER DRIVE
FEMINISM AND RUIN 1 & 2
FIX FOR MISFITS
FOOLS & TRAMPS
FREEDOM SPEAKING
FRENEMY ENABLER
FRENEMY LIAR
FRENEMY THIEF
FRENEMY TRAITOR
TRENEMY TYRANT
GENIUS IS HELD DOWN
GLOBALISLAM
GOD USES THE FLAWED
HAZE OF THE LATTER DAYS

THE HERD IN WORDS
HIX POLITIX
HOW THEY RUINED US
JUST SKIP DINNER
LE FEMME AND THE COMMUNIST SPIRIT
LIBERAL CHAOS & ROT
LIBERAL DOUBLETHINK
LIBERAL GALL 1 & 2
LIBERAL SHOVE-DOWNS
LOCK YOUR GATE
LOSERS and Femme Fatales
MANUAL FOR SUPERIOR MEN
MODERN ART FROM HELL
MOSTLY FAKE
NOTES TO CHAMPS 1 & 2
OVERCOME FRENEMIES
PC MAKES US CRAZY
PEOPLE ARE CRUEL
PEOPLE PROBLEMS 1 & 2
PERSECUTED GENIUIS
POLI-PSYCH MYSTERIES
PRETENTIOUS SLOBS
QUEEN BEE
RED NEW DEAL
RETURNING TO FIRST NATURE
SEASON OF TREASON
SEPARATE MEANS HOLY
SOCIAL HYPNOTISM
SOLITUDE SOLUTION
SUPERCILIOUS
THE SCHOOLS SCREWED EM UP
TOAD TO PRINCE
TRIALS CYCLES
TRUMP VS. GROUP
TRUST IN TRASH
THE TRUTH ABOUT PEOPLE
UNDERHEANDEDLY CLEVER
WALK TALL WITHIN WALLS
WE'RE NOT ALL ONE
WINNERS SKIP DINNER
WORK OR SMERK

KAREN KELLOCK PH.D.

M.S. Political Science, San Diego State. Ph.D. in Psychology, University of California Irvine. Postdoctoral: UCI School of Medicine, Dept. of Psychiatry [NIMH Grants]. Developed the Debris Theory of Disease, a theory of system pathology in 120 books and 22 textbooks for the general public. The theory has a general formula: All disease is obstruction, all recovery is elimination, all success is attraction. The three obstructions are people, habit and food. Remove obstruction and snap to your goals, waiting in the wings.